BASEBALL LEGENDS

Hank Aaron

Grover Cleveland Alexander

Ernie Banks

Albert Belle

Johnny Bench

Yogi Berra

Barry Bonds

Roy Campanella

Roger Clemens

Roberto Clemente

Ty Cobb

Dizzy Dean

Joe DiMaggio

Bob Feller

Lou Gehrig

Bob Gibson

Ken Griffey, Jr.

Rogers Hornsby

Randy Johnson

Walter Johnson

Chipper Jones

Sandy Koufax

Life in the Minor Leagues

Greg Maddux

Mickey Mantle

Christy Mathewson

Willie Mays

Mark McGwire

Stan Musial

Mike Piazza

Cal Ripken, Jr.

Brooks Robinson

Frank Robinson

Jackie Robinson

Pete Rose

Babe Ruth

Nolan Ryan

Mike Schmidt

Tom Seaver

Duke Snider

Warren Spahn

Casey Stengel

Frank Thomas

Honus Wagner

Larry Walker

Ted Williams

Carl Yastrzemski

Cy Young

CHELSEA HOUSE PUBLISHERS

MARK
McGWIRE

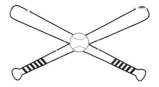

Carrie Muskat

Introduction by
Jim Murray

Senior Consultant
Earl Weaver

CHELSEA HOUSE PUBLISHERS
Philadelphia

Produced by Choptank Syndicate, Inc.

Editor and Picture Researcher: Norman L. Macht
Production Coordinator and Editorial Assistant: Mary E. Hull
Design and Production: Lisa Hochstein

CHELSEA HOUSE PUBLISHERS

Editor in Chief: Stephen Reginald
Managing Editor: James Gallagher
Production Manager: Pamela Loos
Art Director: Sara Davis
Director of Photography: Judy L. Hasday
Senior Production Editor: Lisa Chippendale
Publishing Coordinator: James McAvoy
Cover Design and Digital Illustration: Keith Trego

Cover Photos: AP/Wide World Photos

The Chelsea House World Wide Web site
address is http://www.chelseahouse.com

First Printing

1 3 5 7 9 8 6 2

Library of Congress Cataloging-in-Publication Data

Muskat, Carrie
        Mark McGwire / Carrie Muskat; introduction by Jim Murray
            64 p.   cm.— (Baseball legends)
        Includes bibliographical references (p. 61) and index.
        Summary: Presents a biography of the St. Louis Cardinal power hitter
who broke Roger Maris' single-season home run record in 1998.
        ISBN 0-7910-5155-2 (hc)
        1. McGwire, Mark, 1963– —Juvenile literature. 2. Baseball players—United States—
Biography—Juvenile literature.
        [1. McGwire, Mark, 1963– . 2. Baseball players.] I. Title. II. Series.
        GV865.M387M87 1999
        796.357'092— dc21   98-51065
                                                                                                    CIP
                                                                                                    AC

CONTENTS

WHAT MAKES A STAR

Jim Murray

No one has ever been able to explain to me the mysterious alchemy that makes one man a .350 hitter and another player, more or less identical in physical makeup, hard put to hit .200. You look at an Al Kaline, who played with the Detroit Tigers from 1953 to 1974. He was pale, stringy, almost poetic-looking. He always seemed to be struggling against a bad case of mononucleosis. But with a bat in his hands, he was King Kong. During his career, he hit 399 home runs, rapped out 3,007 hits, and compiled a .297 batting average.

Form isn't the reason. The first time anybody saw Roberto Clemente step into the batter's box for the Pittsburgh Pirates, the best guess was that Clemente would be back in Double A ball in a week. He had one foot in the bucket and held his bat at an awkward angle—he looked as though he couldn't hit an outside pitch. A lot of other ballplayers may have had a better-looking stance. Yet they never led the National League in hitting in four different years, the way Clemente did.

Not every ballplayer is born with the ability to hit a curveball. Nor is exceptional hand-eye coordination the key to heavy hitting. Big league locker rooms are filled with players who have all the attributes, save one: discipline. Every baseball man can tell you a story about a pitcher who throws a ball faster than anyone has ever seen but who has no control on or *off* the field.

The Hall of Fame is full of people who transformed themselves into great ballplayers by working at the sport, by studying the game, and making sacrifices. They're overachievers—and winners. If you want to find them, just watch the World Series. Or simply read about New York Yankee great Lou Gehrig; Ted Williams, "the Splendid Splinter" of the Boston Red Sox; or the Dodgers' strikeout king, Sandy Koufax.

A pitcher *should* be able to win a lot of ballgames with a 98-miles-per-hour fastball. But what about the pitcher who wins 20 games a year with a fastball so slow that you can catch it with your teeth? Bob Feller of the Cleveland Indians got into the Hall of Fame with a blazing fastball that glowed in the dark. National League star Grover Cleveland Alexander got there with a pitch that took considerably longer to reach the plate; but when it did arrive, the pitch was exactly where Alexander wanted it to be—and the last place the batter expected it to be.

There are probably more players with exceptional ability who didn't make it to the major leagues than there are who did. A number of great hitters, bored with fielding practice, had to be dropped from their team because their home-run production didn't make up for their lapses in the field. And then there are players like Brooks Robinson of the Baltimore Orioles, who made himself into a human vacuum cleaner at third base because he knew that working hard to become an expert fielder would win him a job in the big leagues.

A star is not something that flashes through the sky. That's a comet. Or a meteor. A star is something you can steer ships by. It stays in place and gives off a steady glow; it is fixed, permanent. A star works at being a star.

And that's how you tell a star in baseball. He shows up night after night and takes pride in how brightly he shines. He's Willie Mays running so hard his hat keeps falling off; Ty Cobb sliding to stretch a single into a double; Lou Gehrig, after being fooled in his first two at-bats, belting the next pitch off the light tower because he's taken the time to study the pitcher. Stars never take themselves for granted. That's why they're stars.

1

SIXTY-TWO

On a bright, sun-splashed Labor Day, September 7, 1998, the St. Louis Cardinals were playing host to their rivals, the Chicago Cubs. Busch Stadium was a sea of red—red shirts, red hats, red pants, red socks. In an upper deck section of left field, fans not only wore red but also bright yellow hard hats in anticipation of hard-hit home runs. Almost everybody had a camera. Nearly everyone in the left field seats had a glove. If not, they were probably out of luck.

Mark McGwire, the big redheaded first baseman with the 20-inch biceps, had hit his 60th home run two days earlier, to pull even with Babe Ruth, whose single-season home run mark had stood until 1961 when a quiet outfielder named Roger Maris hit 61.

McGwire was not the only one chasing Ruth and Maris in 1998. Cubs outfielder Sammy Sosa trailed Big Mac by two homers heading into their two-game series. There was no animosity between the two sluggers. Both cheered each other on. "I'm a fan of the game as well as a player and I absolutely enjoy watching him play," McGwire said of Sosa. "He is having an absolutely magical

Mark McGwire hits his record-breaking 62nd home run of the season against the Chicago Cubs, September 8, 1998, at St. Louis.

Unlike McGwire, the Yankees' Roger Maris had almost nobody rooting for him when he hit 61 home runs in 1961 to break the record set by the popular Babe Ruth in 1927. But McGwire honored Maris's memory by including the Maris family in his celebration when he hit number 62.

year and, you know, I root him on just like anybody else."

"He's 'The Man,'" Sosa said of McGwire.

Roger Maris's six children were in St. Louis for the series. The McGwire and Sosa show drew a national television audience, 700 media members, and the sport's top officials, including Major League Baseball commissioner Bud Selig. Baseball had not had so much excitement for a regular season game since Cal Ripken Jr. broke Lou Gehrig's iron-man streak of 2,130 games in September 1995. Home runs hit in Ruthian fashion had brought people back to the ballpark in droves in the summer of '98. This would be a real-life home run derby, one-on-one, swing for swing. "I think we're motivation for each other a little bit," Sosa said before the series. So far, the two had homered on the same day 20 times.

Sosa was among the thousands of early birds who watched McGwire loosen up in batting practice. Big Mac did not disappoint the souvenir hunters, launching 11 balls into the seats on his 15 swings. He seemed relaxed and ready.

When the game started and Sosa came to bat in the first inning, the crowd of 50,530 gave him a lengthy standing ovation. Sosa tipped his helmet and made his chest-thumping "I love you" two-fingered salute to McGwire, who was at first base. Sosa then popped up into foul territory near first and McGwire neatly caught it.

Journeyman Mike Morgan was pitching for the Cubs that day. He retired the first two batters he faced, and the crowd was on its feet before McGwire even left the on-deck circle. McGwire stepped in against the 39-year-old right-hander. He had the same routine every at-bat. First his right foot, then his left stepped into the batter's box. He scrunched down into a crouch seemingly impossible for a man with such an imposing, muscle-packed physique. The bat would begin poised over his right shoulder. He would take a few half swings, slowly at first, then pick up the pace the way a dog wags its tail faster and faster in anticipation of playtime with its favorite toy.

The bat looked like a toothpick in his hands. He was Hercules in spikes. Baseballs did not stand a chance against Big Mac.

He fouled the first pitch back. About 40,000 flashbulbs popped. He took the second, which was high. The third was just right. McGwire rocketed the 1–1 pitch into the sky, striking a skybox window in the upper reaches of left field. McGwire watched the ball go, waiting for third base umpire Mike Winters to signal fair. Then, Big Mac went into his home run trot, both arms raised and fists clenched. He punched the air in celebration. Busch Stadium erupted in noise.

As McGwire rounded the bases, he received high fives from Cubs first baseman Mark Grace and third baseman Gary Gaetti. Sosa, standing in right field, put his glove under his arm and joined in the applause. McGwire stomped on home plate, pointed to the stands and rushed to grab his 10-year-old son Matthew, who had arrived just before game time from California. No batboy has ever gotten such a hug from a player. "I was down there getting my bat," McGwire said. "He said, 'How you doing?' I gave him a kiss, told him I loved him. The next thing I knew, I hit a home run."

McGwire pointed his right index finger to the sky and touched his heart in tribute to Maris, the man he had matched. "He tapped his heart, like Dad was in his heart," said Kevin Maris.

McGwire's father will never forget the day. September 7 also was John McGwire's 61st birthday. "What better way to say happy birthday," Mark said.

In front of the dugout, McGwire gave teammate Ray Lankford their patented post-homer greeting—a two-fisted high-five followed by a fake punch to the stomach. Cardinals catcher Tom Lampkin, who had superstitiously avoided talking to McGwire after his previous 60 home runs, was on the field with the rest of his teammates in celebration. They were awestruck. "When he comes up," St. Louis outfielder Ron Gant said, "it's like watching one of The Beatles coming along."

The Cardinals played host to the Cubs the next night, September 8. Right-hander Steve Trachsel started for Chicago, which was fighting to stay alive in the National League wild card race.

Before the game, McGwire touched the bat that Maris had used to hit his 61st. It had been brought to St. Louis from the Hall of Fame for McGwire to hold. "I hope you're with me tonight," McGwire said, hoping to connect with Maris.

The magical moment happened quickly in the fourth inning. Trachsel's first pitch to McGwire was a fastball low and inside. McGwire connected, hitting a line drive that just cleared the left field fence 341 feet away. It was his shortest home run of the season, but it was the biggest. McGwire now had 62 home runs and had broken one of baseball's most hallowed records.

"When I hit the ball, I thought it was a line drive and I thought it was going to hit the wall and the next thing I knew, it disappeared,"

McGwire said. "I had to go back and touch [first base]. I can honestly say that's the first time I ever had to go back and do that." First base coach Dave McKay, McGwire's personal batting practice pitcher, pointed to the bag to make sure.

All four Cubs infielders congratulated McGwire as he circled the bases. Son Matthew was waiting again at home plate and McGwire bearhugged the 10-year-old and lifted him into the air three times. Even Sosa came in from right field to salute the new home run king. As both grinned from ear to ear, McGwire gave Sosa the traditional Cardinal home-run ritual punch in the stomach. The two then exchanged Sosa's post-homer message to his mother—a touch to the heart and then the lips.

"It was a sweet, sweet run around the bases," McGwire said. "I was trying to imagine what it

McGwire's son Matthew was on hand as the Cardinals' batboy to see his father make history. "At the start of the season I asked Matt how many home runs he wanted his daddy to hit," McGwire said. "He said '65.'" Here he hugs Matt after hitting number 61.

was going to feel like doing that. I sure as heck was floating. I hope I didn't act foolish, but this was history."

McGwire made sure he recognized that history. He leapt into the stands near the Cardinals dugout and hugged the Maris family. "For him to come up there and do that, let us partake in that moment, it is outstanding and something we will never forget," Roger Maris Jr. said, fighting back tears. Even the city of Fargo, North Dakota, where Roger Maris grew up, congratulated McGwire. The headline in the Fargo *Forum* newspaper on September 9 was, "It's All Yours, Mark."

The city of St. Louis went berserk. No. 62 was posted on windows and foreheads and rooftops. Drivers honked their horns, cheers rose in restaurants, and people danced in the streets. There were 62-cent specials everywhere. It was a summer to remember.

Special balls labeled with an infrared mark were used so major league officials could determine which one was the real home run ball. Sports collectors projected the record-breaking 62nd home run ball to be worth $1 million. Whoever got the ball would be rich.

However, no fan had a chance to catch it. The ball just cleared the left field fence and 22-year-old Tim Forneris of the Busch Stadium grounds crew picked it up. Forneris stuffed the ball into his shirt and ran onto the field with the other stadium employees to pick up the red and white streamers on the field while McGwire rounded the bases. After the game Forneris presented McGwire with the ball. "Mr. McGwire," Forneris said, "I think I have something that belongs to you." The ball was eventually turned over to the Hall of Fame, where it now resides.

"I'm just in awe," St. Louis manager Tony La Russa said. "I felt that was the first time he really put pressure on himself to do it. Before, he'd taken his at-bats as always. If they walked him, they walked him. This time, he wanted to get it done at home."

The Cardinals players wanted to present McGwire with a commemorative plaque, but he hit home runs 61 and 62 so quickly that the trophy was not ready. They did give him a Cardinal-red 1962 Corvette convertible, which McGwire rode in around the ballpark in a post-game lap, waving to the fans who did not want to leave Busch on this magical night. It was a night of goosebumps.

McGwire had erased a record that had stood for 37 years. For the next five days, baseball showered McGwire with compliments and congratulations on his historic achievement.

Mark McGwire had reached his goal but with 19 days left in the season, he felt that "everybody wanted more." The home runs kept exploding. In the last three games he hit five in just 11 at-bats and finished with 70.

"I can't believe I did it," McGwire said. "It's absolutely amazing. It blows me away."

One day during the 1998 season, Mark McGwire found a cap signed by Roger Maris with two numbers "61" on it in his locker. Not until after he had broken Maris's record did he learn that the cap had been left with the Cardinals before Maris died in 1985 to give "to the guy who breaks my record."

2

THE BABE RUTH SYNDROME

Mark McGwire was a large child. "I was chubby. I had a lot of baby fat," he says. Born in Pomona, California, on October 1, 1963, he grew up in nearby Claremont, a middle-class suburb of Los Angeles.

Mark started playing baseball at the age of eight. Two years later, in his first Little League at-bat against a 12-year-old pitcher, he hit a home run over the right field fence.

His father, John, was a dentist who trained as an amateur boxer. The elder McGwire pounded a speed bag in the garage to stay in shape. As a child he had been bedridden with an illness that left one leg shorter than the other. That did not stop him from playing sports; his determination was an inspiration to his five sons—Mike, Bobby, Mark, Dan, and Jay—all of whom grew to 6'3" or taller.

Mark had a happy childhood playing football, baseball, and basketball with the other kids in the neighborhood. Mark's mother, Ginger, was kept busy with her five boys and their friends, who would enter the McGwire house and help themselves to the well-stocked refrigerator

Mark McGwire was a pitcher in college, but the coach wanted his potent bat in the lineup every day, so Mark played first base and the outfield too.

MARK McGWIRE

During his 45 years at USC, Rod Dedeaux won 11 national titles. One of his players, Hall of Famer Tom Seaver, said of him, "Dedeaux has more enthusiasm for the game than anyone I've been around. He taught me not to make mental mistakes, not to beat yourself."

One day Mark was pitching in a Little League game. He walked so many batters he started to cry on the mound. His father, who was a coach on the team, came out to the mound and had Mark change places with the shortstop. When Mark looked in from that position, everything appeared fuzzy. An eye examination revealed that he needed glasses.

Mark's home runs were impressive from the start. His father estimates that the 10-year-old hit about 18 home runs in 30 games. But he was too young to be named to the All-Star team.

Mark attended Damien High School, an all-boys Catholic school, and pitched for the school team. "He was an awesome presence on the mound," said coach Tom Carroll. He was also the team's best hitter.

Carroll did not want Mark to play on days he was not pitching, but Mark's bat was too potent to keep him on the bench. In a 1981 tournament game, Mark had four hits, two of them home runs, and six RBI.

Dick Wiencik, a scout for the Oakland A's who lived near Mark, heard about him from his own kids who hung around Damien High School. But when Wiencik saw McGwire pitch in high school, he marked him down as just average.

The Montreal Expos thought enough of Mark to pick him in the eighth round of the June draft after he graduated from high school. They offered him $8,500 to sign. Mark turned them down and enrolled at the University of Southern California, where the famed Rod Dedeaux was the coach.

Assistant Coach Ron Vaughn became Mark's hitting mentor. In 1982 they went to the Alaskan Summer League where Mark batted .403 for the Anchorage Glacier Pilots. For the next five years

Vaughn voluntarily worked with McGwire on his hitting every winter.

At USC, McGwire was the best pitcher on a staff that included Randy Johnson. But in Mark's third year, Dedeaux switched him to first base. Like Babe Ruth, who was a star pitcher at the beginning of his legendary career, Mark was too good a hitter not to have him in the lineup every day. McGwire led the Pac-10 conference with 32 home runs.

Dick Wiencik kept an eye on McGwire. "Every time I went to a game, he did something well," he recalled. "Most guys who are 6' 5" and 225 pounds are clumsy. He wasn't. He was well-coordinated."

Wiencik looked beyond Mark's size and ability into his character. "Some of the younger scouts are always looking for tools," he said. "It isn't just tools. You've got to have desire and the right attitude. Mark had great potential."

The Athletics had the 10th pick in the first round of the 1984 amateur draft. Wiencik urged them to take the big redhead from USC. But the A's didn't want a first baseman. So Wiencik told them, "He's a third baseman."

To the A's surprise, Mark was still available when Oakland's turn came. They selected him, and offered him a $145,000 signing bonus.

Wiencik went to the McGwire home with a contract and handed Mark's parents his card that said, "An acre of performance is worth a whole world of promise."

In July 1984, the city of Los Angeles hosted the summer Olympic games. Baseball was a demonstration sport and Dedeaux was the U.S. team's coach. McGwire batted cleanup and played first base on the team that had 17 future major leaguers on the roster. But they lost the gold medal game to Japan, 6–3.

The A's assigned McGwire to Modesto in the Class A California League. They had drafted him as a third baseman and that's where they expected him to play. Hampered by a sore hamstring, Mark played in just 16 games, batting .200.

"Everybody was starting to second-guess me because he didn't do well," Wiencik said. "I said I didn't want him to be judged after two months. I put my job and my career and everything on the line for the kid."

In December Mark married Kathy Williamson, whom he had met at USC.

When McGwire returned to Modesto in 1985, Class A California League manager George Mitterwald was not convinced that third base was the right position for him. "I thought it was a joke from the get-go because of his size," Mitterwald said. "There aren't too many 6-foot-5 third

George Mitterwald had played 11 years as a catcher for the Minnesota Twins and Chicago Cubs. As the manager at Modesto, it was his job to make Mark McGwire into a big league third baseman. He quickly realized it was the wrong position for McGwire.

basemen. Mark, for a big guy, was coordinated and had a tremendous arm but as far as throwing, that wasn't his forte."

To play third base, a player needs not only to be coordinated but also to be able to react quickly. "Brooks Robinson wasn't a fast runner but his first step was quick and his hands were quick," Mitterwald said. "A big guy like Mark, they're usually not that quick."

Mitterwald stuck with the organization's plan for nearly two months. Then he switched McGwire to first base. "He's such a big target, you can hardly throw a ball over his head," Mitterwald said.

The one adjustment college players have to make when they join the pros is switching from an aluminum bat to a wooden one. McGwire was no exception.

"His bat was slow," Mitterwald said. "But he was so big, people pitched him away and with that aluminum bat, he could reach out and boom, it was gone. With the wooden bat, he had to generate more bat speed. He developed a short, quick compact swing. But at first, he had this long, loopy swing. He struggled a little bit."

At the plate, the big redhead would stand way back in the batter's box. Mitterwald tried to convince McGwire to move up in the box. "I wanted him close enough that he would have to learn how to handle the inside fastball—and he fought it."

Mitterwald was a lifetime .236 hitter. But Bob Watson, the A's roving hitting instructor, had a career .295 average. So when Watson came to Modesto and said, "Hey, Mark, did you ever think about moving up to home plate?" McGwire paid attention.

"Yeah, that sounds like a pretty good idea," he said.

McGwire stepped up in the batter's box that day and hit two home runs. "Sometimes," Mitterwald said, "it takes someone else to come in and reinforce what you've been trying to teach."

For all his size, McGwire was a gentle giant. "He was playing third base one day and somebody hit a shot right at him. He caught it and came back to the dugout and said, 'Man, that was a toughie wuffie.' Here's this 6-foot-5 guy saying that," Mitterwald said.

"Right out of college, his legs were big but not strong," Mitterwald said. "He had baby fat on his legs. He didn't have much of a chest. His forearms were nothing like they are now. He wasn't near as strong. Still, he did hit some balls back then a long way."

McGwire batted .274 in 138 games at Modesto with 50 extra-base hits, including 24 homers, and 106 RBI. He was chosen the 1985 California League Rookie of the Year. He started the 1986 season with the Huntsville Stars of the Class AA Southern League, and moved up to Tacoma of the AAA Pacific Coast League on June 6. McGwire hit .311 with 23 homers and 112 RBI in the minors that year.

"I think he started picking up his bat speed when he started moving up in baseball," Mitterwald said. "Just Mark's own makeup and his ability to learn things and apply it to his own physical abilities helped him get that much quicker."

On August 20, 1986, McGwire was called up to the big league A's. He made his debut two days later, and on August 24 collected his first major league hit off New York Yankees pitcher Tommy

John. The next day at Tiger Stadium in Detroit, he hit his first home run, a towering shot that cleared the 440-foot sign in center field off pitcher Walt Terrell in an 8–4 Oakland win.

McGwire never really got settled with Oakland, hitting .189 with 10 hits and three homers in 53 at-bats. Oakland had switched him back to third base and fielding was a problem. He made six errors in 16 games.

But Oakland manager Tony La Russa knew the A's had something special. "The three most vivid characteristics were an outstanding arm, real short, quick arm. He had good hands for a big guy. You could see it defensively," La Russa said. "But mostly, he had this very compact stroke that he could repeat over and over again. It was so sound, you thought, 'Wow.' He had such a fundamentally sound stroke and he used the whole field, you thought he had the chance to be very special."

3

ROOKIE OF
THE YEAR

McGwire learned that it took more than 20-inch biceps to hit home runs. "What I know now, I wish I had when I was younger," he said. "Hitting is mental. That's all it is. It's not your physical ability, it's how strong your mind is. It controls everything you want to do. The problem is a lot of people don't use it."

Rob Nelson was penciled in as Oakland's regular first baseman for the 1987 season and Mark McGwire was scheduled to play one more season in the minors at the Triple-A level. But in spring training, A's manager Tony La Russa had a chance to watch McGwire every day.

"He was so exciting," La Russa said, "We kept him and Robby Nelson was sent down."

McGwire hit some impressive homers early in his rookie year. During a three-game stretch in Detroit May 8–10, McGwire hit five homers. In a three-game series at Cleveland June 26–28, he hit five more, drove in seven runs, and scored runs in nine consecutive at-bats.

On June 28 McGwire slugged three homers to lead the A's in a 13–3 rout of Cleveland, raising his season total to 25, one behind American League leader George Bell of Toronto.

McGwire was quickly becoming "The Man" in Oakland. "It was 'Wow,'" said longtime Oakland broadcaster Bill King, who watched McGwire emerge in his rookie season.

McGwire could not understand all the attention he was getting and had to be coaxed into

McGwire and outfielder Jose Canseco became known as the "Bash Brothers" when they hit 80 home runs between them in 1987. Not content with high fives, they bashed their massive forearms in salute. Off the field, they were complete opposites in personality and lifestyle.

answering reporters' questions. Big Mac didn't think he was doing anything special. McGwire and outfield teammate Jose Canseco were both hitting homers at an incredible pace and were quickly dubbed the "Bash Brothers."

Canseco was boisterous and loved the attention his powerful home runs created while McGwire was quiet and almost shy. "At the time, he didn't know how special he was," said teammate Dennis Eckersley. "I guess he was just naturally green."

"I think he was green," catcher Terry Steinbach said, "but he was very, very confident."

Steinbach and McGwire were roommates in 1987 because the A's wanted the two rookies to learn the big leagues together. "I can remember spring training and making the club, and thinking, 'Wow, there are future Hall of Famers here,'" Steinbach said. "You're so wide eyed. Once we got over that, it was, 'Hey, I'm a part of this team.' All of those guys were very willing to communicate and it was easy for us to sit back and be like a sponge and take in the experiences they had and how they handled them."

The veteran players advised the young players about the need to pace themselves over the 162-game season. The rookies had the energy and enthusiasm to keep the older players excited about each day's game. "I think we fed off each other," Steinbach said.

McGwire started to direct some of his energy toward weight lifting. Dave McKay, an Oakland coach, guided the players to the gym. The key, McKay said, was to do exercises that would make them better athletes, not lift Mack trucks. Many critics felt if players lifted weights, they would become too big and muscular. McKay made sure they did it right.

"That doesn't make you hit the ball," McGwire said of being bulked up. "Good hand-to-eye coordination does, and the man upstairs gives you good timing to do that. You're born with the ability to be a home run hitter. You're born with good genetics, good parents. I thank my parents for that. I can't tell you anybody who says he lifts weights and that's why he became a home run hitter. There are guys that lift weights way more than I do that don't hit home runs."

On August 14 McGwire hit the first pitch from California Angels pitcher Don Sutton in the sixth inning for his 39th homer to set a major league rookie record.

McGwire finished with 49, tops in the American League and tied with the Chicago Cubs' Andre Dawson for best in the majors. He might have had a chance at 50 but missed the last game to be with his wife at the birth of their son, Matthew. To McGwire some things were more important than home runs.

Despite the numbers, McGwire insisted he wasn't a home run hitter. "He'd say, 'I'm an alley to alley line-drive hitter and the ball goes out sometimes,'" broadcaster Bill King said of the unanimous Rookie of the Year choice.

"Everyone wants to know how many home runs McGwire will hit this year," La Russa said before the 1988 season. "It's the worst question. Nobody knows. Home runs are strange things. He may hit 49 again. Or it might be less. It doesn't matter. He's a solid hitter. It's the runs batted in that's important."

Pitchers made adjustments in 1988. Mac finished with 32 homers and 99 RBI. Canseco hit 42 and drove in 124. The A's posted a 104–58 record, the best in baseball, and won the American League West by 13 games. They swept Boston in four games in the American League Championship Series (ALCS); McGwire batted .333 with a home run and three RBI.

But the Los Angeles Dodgers won the World Series in five games. McGwire's game-winning ninth-inning home run in Game 3 was his only hit of the Series.

Just before the Series, Mark and his wife had separated; they were later divorced.

In 1989 the A's were on a mission to erase the bad feelings of that World Series loss. McGwire was no longer green; he was in a groove. He led the American League with a home run every 14.8 at-bats and totaled 33. Mac drove in 95 runs, 10th best in the league, despite missing some time in early April because of a herniated disc in his back.

"We had a belief that we were going to win every game," said Art Kusnyer, an Oakland coach. The A's continued their rampage in the American League West and finished 99–63, the best record in baseball for the second consecutive year. Backed by the solid pitching of 21-game winner Dave Stewart, Mike Moore, and Bob Welch, Oakland crushed Toronto 4–1 to win the ALCS and advanced to the World Series against the San Francisco Giants.

The A's won the first two games of the "Series by the Bay," but on October 17 an earthquake that rocked northern California abruptly interrupted Game 3 at Candlestick Park. "I thought it was a five-pointer, a little one," said McGwire, who had experienced several quakes. "I was

Babe Ruth (left) and Lou Gehrig were the original Bash Brothers. In 1927 the Yankee sluggers hit 107—60 for Ruth and 47 for Gehrig.

Mark McGwire (25) and other A's stand stunned, watching fans leave the Oakland Coliseum after an earthquake hit northern California just before the start of Game 3 of the 1989 World Series on October 17. The Series resumed 10 days later after the stadium was declared sound.

standing next to Canseco. He threw his bat down, and my first reaction was, 'I know he's strong, but I didn't think his bat was that powerful.' Then I felt my knees and legs buckle, and I saw things moving, and I knew it was an earthquake."

Ten days later the Series resumed at Candlestick, and the fans responded. A crowd of 62,038 watched Oakland win 13–7, crushing five home runs against the Giants. "We had death and we had destruction," Stewart said before taking the mound. "It was a time when you had to test yourselves, find out what you're really about . . . and you have to go on."

San Francisco could not stop the A's, whose 9–6 win completed the sweep.

In 1990 the A's won the American League West for the third consecutive year with a 103–59 record. McGwire led the team with 108 RBI. He also earned respect for his glove work, making just five errors and winning his first Rawlings Gold Glove for defensive excellence at first base. He gave the Gold Glove trophy to his optometrist.

The A's swept the Red Sox in the ALCS, then were swept themselves by Cincinnati in the World Series. The Bash Brothers were blushing in embarrassment. McGwire had three singles in 14 at-bats. Canseco went 1-for-12. "We got what we earned," La Russa said after the sweep.

4

NOW BATTING, NO. 25, SUPERMAN

Tony La Russa (right) was Mark McGwire's manager in Oakland. When La Russa moved to the St. Louis Cardinals, McGwire soon followed him. Like everybody else in baseball, La Russa was awed by McGwire's super season. "You have to laugh or cry. You have to do something extraordinary," La Russa said after McGwire hit number 70. "In 19 years, I've never kissed a player. But I kissed him."

Mark McGwire had four tremendous seasons with the Oakland Athletics from 1987 to 1990. And then there was 1991. "He had a really bad year," A's manager Tony La Russa said. "He was very embarrassed professionally and personally."

In 1991 McGwire batted .201, hit 22 home runs, and drove in 75 runs. He had cut back on his weight-lifting program. Before the final game of the season, he asked La Russa to keep him out of the lineup. "I'm scared to death," McGwire told La Russa. "I don't want to hit below .200. I don't think I could handle it." La Russa complied.

"He'd lost all his confidence," Mark's father said.

McGwire called it a "wake-up season." When it ended he called the A's employee assistance department and told them he needed help. He began seeing a therapist. "The counseling started as a personal thing, but before long it was everything—personal, professional, dealing with the media, dealing with fans, dealing with life," McGwire said. "I got my mind straight, and everything followed.

"When you feel good about yourself physically," McGwire said, "you'll feel good about yourself mentally. When I didn't lift in '91, I was a basket case mentally. And when I started lifting again, when I started seeing changes in my body and started getting serious about it, it's amazing how things in your physical body, how looking in the mirror and seeing changes, how it changes your mental approach in anything."

In 1992 the real Mark McGwire returned. He led the major leagues by averaging one home run every 11.1 at-bats. With 38 homers on August 21, McGwire had a six-homer lead over Texas slugger Juan Gonzalez, but he strained a muscle on the right side of his rib cage that night at Camden Yards in Baltimore and had to go on the disabled list.

He finished with 42 home runs, second to Gonzalez's 43, batted .268, 67 points higher than 1991, and led the team with 104 RBI.

The A's, who had finished fourth in 1991, won the AL West in '92 with a 96–66 record but lost to Toronto in the American League Championship Series in six games. McGwire hit a two-run homer off Jack Morris in his first at-bat of the Series but finished 2-for-19 with one RBI.

For McGwire, the next two years were all but wiped out by injuries. A sore left heel limited him to 27 games in 1993. Back stiffness and a stress fracture of his left heel kept him out of all but 47 games in the strike-shortened '94 season.

The layoff gave McGwire more time in the gym. He stayed in the Oakland area to train, dedicating himself to getting in the best shape of his life. He reduced his 20 percent body fat by more than half. He improved his diet, ran regularly for the first time, and worked out on an exercise bike. The transformation involved more than his physique. The shy McGwire, now 31, was becoming more outspoken.

"I've always been the type of person where I like people to learn from me by the way I play instead of the way I talk," he said. "But there comes a certain time in your career, your life, where you have enough experience that you might have something to say to somebody and they might listen.

"I feel really good personally, which I think reflects on how I feel playing the game," he said. "You have to feel good inside and then I think everything else falls into place. It's just a matter of getting everything in tune."

The injuries in 1993 and '94 also gave McGwire time to study the game.

"It's sad to think that sometimes it takes failure to make you change things but it does," said McGwire, who began studying pitchers and taking preparations more seriously. La Russa saw the transformation firsthand. "Early on, he was a tremendous talent, but the thing that worried you a little was that he really wanted to keep it simple," La Russa said. "A lot of times he didn't want to know who was pitching. He just wanted to go up there, see it and swing at it."

McGwire arrived in Arizona in March 1995 to work out with his A's teammates while they waited for the labor situation to be resolved. He kept in touch with Terry Steinbach, his former rookie roommate and the Oakland player representative, and spoke out against ownership. McGwire claimed baseball's owners were trying to break the players union. La Russa was surprised at Mac's outburst.

"I think the problem is that I've never spoken up in the nine years I've been with Oakland and now I'm speaking up and I don't think people know how to handle it," McGwire said. "Some people

McGwire takes as much pride in his fielding as his home runs. Despite his aching feet or back, he took ground balls every day that he could. "What he can do is amazing for a big man," said second baseman Mike Gallego. "He's got that range of a second baseman, he's flexible, and he's not just a big mountain that can't move."

don't think I have a brain. They think I only play baseball."

McGwire posted his first two-homer game of the season on June 10 at Boston and followed that by hitting three the next day. The first homer was estimated at 463 feet, the longest hit out of Fenway Park at that point in the season. The second was 411 feet, just over the Green Monster's right edge in center field. The third was 452 feet, the second longest hit at Fenway.

"It's a treat to watch a day like that," said Oakland's Scott Brosius. "They were just majestic home runs. They're not just home runs with him, they've got a lot of hang time and air time. There aren't too many who can hit them like that."

"Today, No. 25 was Superman," said Oakland pitcher Todd Stottlemyre.

The five home runs in consecutive games tied a major league record, which he already shared. McGwire and Ralph Kiner were the only players to do so twice. "That's a beautiful thing," Boston's Mo Vaughn said of McGwire. "We try to get five [homers] a month and he got five in two days." The Boston fans, in awe after McGwire's effort June 10, arrived early the next day to watch Big Mac take batting practice.

Vaugn and McGwire were tied for the major league lead with 24 homers and 59 RBI each when McGwire was hit in the helmet by a David Cone pitch on July 8. He sustained a mild concussion and missed the All-Star Game in Arlington, Texas. Cone, pitching for Toronto at the time, said he didn't intend to hit McGwire, who was hit by a pitch 11 times that season.

"I don't think it matters if it was intentional or not," McGwire said. "The fact is he hit me in the head. It's like a drunk driver saying he didn't mean to hit the little kid who was crossing the street."

The season already was shortened to 144 games because of the strike, and McGwire lost another 33 because of a bruised left foot and sore back. Still, he finished the year with 39 home runs in 317 at-bats.

The times were changing for the Oakland Athletics. Steve Schott headed a new ownership group that took over the team from the Haas family on November 1, 1995, and warned that they would have to trim payroll from $35 million to $25 million. That meant, Schott said, they might have to trade players like McGwire or Steinbach.

Then came the shocking news that La Russa was leaving Oakland to manage the St. Louis Cardinals. McGwire offered to go with his manager. "I'd be thrilled to death to play for him again," McGwire said. "It would be great. We have such close ties, he knows how I play and I know how he manages."

La Russa also respected his talented first baseman. "Teammates always wanted to go to dinner with him," La Russa said. "There was always laughter in the clubhouse. One thing I've always said about Mark is that if you're a comedian, you should pay him to be in the audience. I don't think I've ever been around a guy who enjoys a joke as much as Mark. He has a terrific sense of humor.

"He was always such a good teammate, always interacted well and was never standoffish. He didn't enjoy the spotlight. He hit 49 [homers] and was a big star. The next year, he hit 30. He enjoyed every opportunity he could to blend into the background and let the other guys who were more colorful take it on."

In March 1996, McGwire was once again sidelined with the same injury to his left heel that had cost him 250 games in 1993–94. "I was so tired of having to do rehab that I just wanted to walk away from it," McGwire said. "But I was talked out of it by family and friends. Nobody plays their career totally perfect. There's always some adversity."

When he was activated April 23, he made up for missed time. On May 17 at Boston, McGwire started a stretch in which he hit 21 homers in 36 games. He belted his 300th career home run on June 25 off Detroit's Omar Olivares. During the month of June, McGwire hit .329 with 25 RBI and a .915 slugging percentage. He rarely had a cheap home run. On July 24, he hit a 470-foot rocket at Comiskey Park. The next day in Toronto, he homered into the fifth deck of SkyDome, a 488-foot shot.

"He just simplifies it," Oakland teammate Jason Giambi said. "It's 'Hey, I see the ball, I hit the ball and it goes 527 feet.' Not many people can hit the ball that far."

McGwire finished the '96 season with a major league-leading 52 home runs, hitting them at a record rate of one every 8.13 at-bats.

"He hits home runs like I hit singles," Giambi said. "He has perfected the art of hitting a home run. I wasn't around with Babe Ruth and I've seen tapes of Mickey Mantle, but he by far is the greatest home run hitter to ever live."

5

JUST A BIG KID

Mark McGwire's physique changed over the years. "It's really amazing a person could be that committed," said Terry Steinbach. "A lot of players know they have to work out—they don't like it, but they know they have to because otherwise it will affect their performance. He enjoys working out. He enjoys going to the gym."

McGwire developed 20-inch biceps, but it wasn't just from lifting weights. He learned about nutrition and watched what he ate, reducing his body fat. His teammates marveled at his meals. Some days were "red meat" days and McGwire would eat a baked potato and two steaks. The next day it might be two big bowls of pasta. He researched nutritional supplements and started using creatine, which helped his strength, reduced his body fat, and helped his muscles recover. Some major league teams had advised their players not to use creatine, since no one was sure what the side effects were. "The problem people have with it," McGwire said, "is when people abuse it. Anything you abuse isn't good for you."

Jason Giambi, 6' 2" first baseman, had joined the A's in 1995. He and McGwire quickly became

Mark McGwire was often compared to another baseball strongman, Jimmie Foxx. "He's just an awesome physical specimen," Houston hitting coach Tom McCraw said. "He gets power anywhere he wants to. He can pull it out of his toes if he wants."

friends. Before every game, they would go to a batting cage to do their daily hitting drill. One of the Oakland coaches would get down on one knee and flip a ball underhand to one of the two behemoths. The timing drill helped them get loose as well as discipline themselves. It also helped McGwire focus.

"He likes flips because every day when he puts in his contacts, it helps him track the ball," said Giambi. "He's had so many back problems, it's one of the ways he gets loose."

Spending time with McGwire made Giambi realize how hard the big redhead worked. "It's like with Michael Jordan," Giambi said of the Chicago Bulls star guard. "People don't know that he has to go out and shoot forever. They think he just shows up and that's it. It's the same with Mark. He doesn't just show up and hit 500-foot homers. He constantly works year round."

McGwire had to keep working to counter his back problems caused by a bulging disc. He had to do daily exercises, but it was part of the discipline he had developed in his life.

"Physical strength obviously helps. But it also hurts," Steinbach said. "There are a lot of guys in the league who have gotten big and strong and all of a sudden their production and endurance and stamina have gone down. Baseball is so much mental, whatever makes you feel mentally right is what you should do."

Pitchers struggled to find ways to stop the Big Mac attack. Anaheim pitcher Chuck Finley said, "Mac generates a lot of bat speed. A guy's size doesn't really bother a pitcher. It's the bat speed they create that hurts you. Mac's got a lot of speed through the bottom of the zone."

McGwire's home runs remained impressive. On April 20 in Detroit, he became the fourth player to clear the left field roof at Tiger Stadium with a 514-foot homer. On June 24 he hit the longest in Seattle's Kingdome history—538 feet— off hard-throwing left-hander Randy Johnson.

"Over the years he's gotten stronger and has more knowledge of the strike zone," said Jose Canseco. "I have seen him get better and better every year. . . . I really noticed it when I was away for a few years and came back. You get spoiled watching him every day. In my opinion, he is the best power hitter that's ever been, and I'm talking about Babe Ruth and Hank Aaron in their prime. He can catch them all if he plays another 10 years, but I don't know if he'll want to."

McGwire's bashes sparked talk about the magic number 61, the record set by the late Roger Maris in 1961. "It's still too early to tell for that," said McGwire, who was the first major-leaguer to reach 30 that year. "It's been a lot of hard work, but we've got a long way to go."

McGwire expected to be wearing an A's uniform for the rest of his career, but rumors were flying that he would be traded. He had not disguised his growing frustration with the team's direction.

"It was killing him inside to come to the park every day and try to find things to play for," Giambi said.

The A's faced a bleak choice between watching McGwire leave as a free agent after the 1997 season, or trading him. The decision was made easier for them by Cardinals manager Tony La Russa, who wanted McGwire for his team.

On July 31, McGwire was traded to the Cardinals for three pitchers. "I think probably the weirdest thing will be putting on red shoes," McGwire joked.

The remaining A's were left wondering how they would survive.

"He's our offense," outfielder Matt Stairs said. "Thirty-four home runs and 81 RBI—you can't replace that. And the heck with numbers, Mark's just a great person and a great friend."

The blockbuster deal would not have happened if it weren't for McGwire's son Matthew, who was nine. Matthew was living in Orange County, California, with his mother, Kathy, whom McGwire had divorced in 1988. It was difficult for McGwire to be an absentee father. He did not like the idea of being farther away from his son and would not give the A's the go-ahead on the deal until he talked to Matthew. His son said yes to St. Louis.

"It's scary how much alike we are," McGwire said of Matthew, who gets a seat on the team plane when he travels with his dad. "I don't have to say a word to him sometimes because he knows what I'm thinking."

McGwire's arrival in St. Louis was the baseball event of the year in a city that takes baseball seriously. In the second at-bat of his Busch Stadium debut on August 8 against Philadelphia, McGwire hit a 441-foot drive off the left field foul pole at the Stadium Club level.

The Cardinals opened three of the seven Busch Stadium gates two hours before game time so fans could see players take their swings. McGwire hit in the last group, and on his first night at Busch, a reported 5,000 fans showed up to watch him. "It's a lot different than California, that's for sure," said pitcher Dennis Eckersley, who was pitching for the Cardinals in 1997. "Even when we were good in Oakland, they didn't have that kind of appreciation."

"Any great baseball town would love McGwire," La Russa said. "But people in St. Louis really take to good people. Once they found out Mark had a human side it was all over."

Five weeks after the trade, McGwire called his attorney Robert Cohen. Mac wanted to stay in St. Louis. Cohen tried to get McGwire to wait and test the free agent market after the season but McGwire said no. On September 16 the Cardinals and McGwire called a news conference to announce he had signed a three year contract extension that guaranteed him $30 million. He

McGwire had always been uncomfortable as the center of attention. But he endured the unending questions and interviews with grace and good humor throughout his amazing season. "I don't think of myself as anything special," he said. "I'm a normal person who has a talent to play this game."

was to get an additional $1 for every ticket sold beyond 2.8 million.

Besides the new deal, McGwire announced he was establishing a foundation to aid abused and neglected children. He would donate $1 million a year to the cause. Through a friend, McGwire had become aware of the incredible and devastating number of abused children and wanted to do something about it. When asked about his concern during the news conference, McGwire suddenly was overcome. The stories and the faces of the children, many the same age as his own son, flashed in his head. He broke down and cried.

"I surprised myself," McGwire said. "I didn't know all that emotion was going to come out."

Eckersley was not surprised by the tears.

"He's a big kid," Eckersley said of his team- mate. "He cares about kids. I look at Mac and it makes me think that I have to remember to be a kid again. You don't want to lose that kid in you, especially when you're playing this game."

McGwire's foundation efforts are heartfelt. "The money we make in baseball is so ridiculous, how can you not do something like that? When you do it, you think, 'What a great feeling,'" he said.

That day, the Cardinals were playing the Los Angeles Dodgers at Busch Stadium. When McGwire walked to the plate, he was greeted by a standing ovation. He responded by hitting a 517-foot blast off the facade above the left center field scoreboard, the longest homer ever measured at Busch. The home run was his 52nd of the sea- son, matching his previous single season high.

McGwire hit six more homers to finish with 58 for the season, tying the record for right-handed sluggers. Only Babe Ruth had hit 50 or more homers in consecutive seasons before McGwire.

"He is a freak," said St. Louis catcher Tom Pagnozzi. "There are power hitters and then there is Mark McGwire. He's way beyond anybody else in this game. I've been in St. Louis 11 years and I saw him hit more balls into the upper deck in two months than all the other players in all my years there combined."

One of the most popular T-shirts in the Cardinals clubhouse was a picture of a can of spinach. The back of the shirt read: "If Popeye wants his arms back, he'll just have to wait until after October. —Mark McGwire."

Pagnozzi even went so far as to ask pitching coach Dave Duncan to reschedule their pregame meeting times. The pitchers and catchers were going over their game strategy while McGwire was taking batting practice.

"We want to see Mark hit," Pagnozzi said. Duncan gladly made the change.

Everyone wanted to see Mark McGwire hit.

6
LET THE COUNTDOWN BEGIN

The questions started early in 1998. Could Mark McGwire break Roger Maris's record of 61 homers in a single season? McGwire did his best to downplay the expectations. "There's no reason to talk about it," McGwire said in January while attending the St. Louis Cardinals' fan convention. "I can't say I'm going to do it, I can't say I won't. If it happens, it happens. How can it be a goal? I don't know if I'm even going to wake up the next morning. As long as I wake up and put my 10 toes on the ground, I'm happy.

"I really believe hitting home runs is a God-given talent," McGwire said on the eve of the season opener. "Every year, adults ask me, 'Can you teach my son to hit home runs?' And I say, 'No, I can't.' I think you're given the talent. If you want to work on it, then you become a successful baseball player. It's just a tough thing."

The home run countdown began on Opening Day, March 31. The Cardinals were playing host to the Los Angeles Dodgers at Busch Stadium. The bases were loaded in the fifth inning when McGwire came to bat. The fans were on their feet. McGwire launched a changeup from Ramon

After hitting five home runs in his last 11 at-bats to finish with 70, McGwire said, "I can't believe I did it. It's absolutely amazing. It blows me away. . . . It's unheard of for somebody to hit 70 home runs. I'm in awe of myself right now." Here he hits his 70th on September 27th in St. Louis.

Martinez into the left field seats for a grand slam and helped the Cardinals win 6–0. McGwire received the first of what would be many standing ovations. "There's no other place in America that you'd want to play in," McGwire said of the rousing reception.

In the second game, also against the Dodgers, McGwire hit his second homer, a 12th-inning game winner. He homered in the third game and again in the fourth.

"He's the premier power hitter in today's game and possibly of all time," teammate Todd Stottlemyre said. "But yet you wouldn't know it by talking to him. He's not talking about how far he hits the ball, he's not talking about how great he is."

McGwire let his bat do the talking. On April 14, McGwire's 10-year-old son Matthew was in town to be a batboy for the first time. His dad responded big time, hitting three home runs in a 15–5 St. Louis victory.

A strange phenomenon developed early in the season. Fans were not content to wait for Big Mac's home runs. They wanted to see the redhead warm up. In addition to the Cardinals, other teams around the league opened their gates early so folks could watch batting practice. "What I do in BP, I've been doing for 11 years," McGwire said. "Now all of a sudden, it's a feature attraction. But I look at it in the positive sense. If it brings people out to the ballpark, if it helps the game of baseball, then fine. We need it."

Most of McGwire's home runs were launched like rockets, soaring so high it seemed as if they would never come down. On May 16, he whacked a ball 545 feet off a Busch Stadium sign in deep center field. Even McGwire was impressed. "It was the best ball I've ever hit," he said. A huge Band-Aid was attached to the sign to mark it.

In May McGwire batted .326 with 16 home runs and posted a .907 slugging percentage in 26 games. Even more incredible was his .513 on-base percentage. Teams were walking him at a record-setting pace, sometimes intentionally with the bases empty.

"I've known the strike zone since I was a kid learning to play baseball," McGwire said. "Sometimes you widen it a little in certain situations, depending on the score of the game and the pitcher—what he's been getting called strikes and balls. The majority of the time I think I'm pretty patient. That's one of the things that was preached to me when I was younger in Oakland— that patience was way more important than your average. And I take pride in that."

Injuries were considered the only obstacles in McGwire's pursuit of the home run record. Trouble flared briefly on June 1 when he took himself out of a game in the first inning against San Diego. He skipped a three-game series against Los Angeles June 2–4 because of lower back spasms. On June 5, his first day back, McGwire silenced any skeptics by hitting No. 28 against San Francisco.

McGwire spent a significant amount of time studying videos of opposing pitchers and visualizing every aspect of his at-bats. "It's not easy," McGwire said. "It's very hard work. I study pitchers. I visualize pitches. That gives me a better chance every time I step into the box. That doesn't mean I'm going to get a hit every game but that's one of the reasons I've come a long way as a hitter."

On the road McGwire resembled a rock star. Fans came in crowds to see him. On June 16 in

"Babe Ruth—what can you say," McGwire said on reaching 60 home runs. "I mean it almost makes you speechless when people put your name alongside his name. . . . Hopefully someday when I pass away, I get to meet him and then I can really truly find out what he was really like."

Houston, 15,000 arrived early for batting practice. Reporters, television cameras, and security guards lined the field from dugout to dugout around the batting cage. Nobody wanted to miss a single swing. "I walked onto the field and there were 18,000 people in the stands for batting practice," St. Louis catcher Tom Pagnozzi said. "I thought I was late for the game. It was like a bad dream."

McGwire was bothered by all the attention. This is a team game, he reminded everyone. Batting practice was "out of control," he said, adding it "was the first time I felt like a caged lion." Practice always begins with a bunt. When McGwire bunted, the fans booed.

In June, McGwire went 18 at-bats without a homer, and then hit the second-longest home run in Cleveland's Jacobs Field history when he smacked his 35th in the first inning. The 462-foot drive dented a crossbeam on a pole connected to the left field scoreboard. Cleveland's Jim Thome said McGwire "is like the Empire State Building standing there with a bat in his hand. Words can't describe how good he is—to keep doing it day after day with the media pressure. I would have liked to see Ruth and him in the same era."

But the Cardinals lost that game to Cleveland and had been outscored 30–6 in their last three games. That bothered McGwire. "It's just not good losing," he said. "I don't think anybody enjoys it. It's just not fun." The increased media attention was no fun either. Wherever he went, McGwire was asked the same questions over and over.

Then suddenly McGwire had company in the home run race. In June, Chicago Cubs outfielder Sammy Sosa hit a one-month record 20 home runs. By July 1, McGwire had 37 and Sosa had 33.

McGwire's pace slowed in July; he hit only eight home runs, a good month's production for anyone else. Sosa kept pace with him. On August 8 the Cubs and Cardinals played at Busch Stadium. McGwire clobbered his 46th, ending a homerless drought of 29 at-bats. Sosa hit his 44th.

Then Sosa got hot. On August 19, against the Cardinals at Wrigley Field, he passed McGwire for the major league lead—for 58 minutes. Sosa hit his 48th home run in the fifth inning but McGwire, who had been homerless in 20 previous at-bats, tied Sosa and the game in the eighth with No. 48, then hit a game-winning 49th in the 10th inning.

McGwire did not show much emotion whenever he homered. He flipped the bat, then followed the path around the bases with a methodical trot. But on August 20 in New York, McGwire pumped his right fist into the air and clapped his hands after hitting home run No. 50. McGwire became the only player to hit at least 50 home runs in three consecutive seasons.

"Obviously, it's history," McGwire said. "There have been thousands of power hitters to play this game, and nobody's ever done it. I can sit here and say I'm the first major league player to ever do it. And I'm pretty proud of it." Maris's record now seemed reachable. "I have to say I do have a shot," McGwire said. "But I know it's going to be tough."

That night, McGwire took boxes of new baseballs back to his hotel room and signed one for every one of his Cardinals teammates. He wrote "50–50–50," the date, personalized it with the player's name, and signed it.

The media scrutiny of McGwire intensified. Even his locker was fair game. Besides batting gloves, packs of sugarless gum and a can of Popeye spinach, there was a bottle of Androstenedione, a testosterone-producing pill that was legal in baseball but banned in the National Football League, the Olympics, and the National Collegiate Athletic Association.

McGwire had taken the pill for more than a year. The substance builds lean muscle mass and promotes recovery after injury. It does not improve the hand-eye coordination necessary to hit home runs, though. McGwire did his best to downplay the controversy. "Everything I've done is natural. Everybody that I know in the game of baseball uses the same stuff I use," said McGwire. Sammy Sosa admitted he took a supplement, too. He preferred Flintstone vitamins—"Fred" was his favorite—before games.

McGwire ignored his critics. On September 1, he broke the National League record of 56 set by the Cubs' Hack Wilson in 1930 by blasting a pair of homers into the center field seats at Pro Player Stadium in Miami.

McGwire's 56th came in the seventh inning, a towering shot off Livan Hernandez. "On the first one, four people went to the concession stand to buy hot dogs, put ketchup, mustard, and relish on them and came back before the ball came down," said Florida third base coach Rich Donnelly. Home run No. 57 came in the ninth off a split-finger pitch from reliever Donn Pall. "He's like an 18-year-old playing with a fake birth certificate in our Little League," Pall said.

The next day he hit another pair in the Cardinals' 14–4 victory over Florida. No. 58 was the third longest ever hit at Pro Player Stadium, landing halfway up the upper deck in left at 497 feet. No. 59 traveled only 458 feet.

The question now was not "if" but "when" and McGwire answered that in early September. On September 7, he tied Roger Maris's 61 against the Cubs at St. Louis. The next day he broke the record. Sammy Sosa ran in from his position in right field to congratulate McGwire with a bear hug.

McGwire's 62 reigned for only five days. On September 13, Sammy Sosa hit two to tie him. McGwire hit his 63rd on September 15; Sosa hit a grand slam the next day. McGwire took the lead on the 18th, and added No. 65 two days later. Sosa matched him with a pair on the 25th.

They went into the final weekend of the season tied at 65. In the fourth inning in Houston, Sosa blasted his 66th to take the lead. Forty-five minutes later McGwire hit one out. It was the

Baseball fans everywhere cheered McGwire on his quest, even at the expense of their own teams. Here fans in Cincinnati invite him to hit one in their direction.

The Cubs' Sammy Sosa (left) and McGwire were never jealous of each other during their race for the home run record. They saluted each other every time one of them hit one out. "At the end, whoever is on top, I don't think it really matters," McGwire said at this pregame news conference on Labor Day, when McGwire had 60 and Sosa 58. "Wouldn't it be great if we just ended tied?" Asked how many would be a good number for a tie, he said, "Seventy." Sosa finished with 66.

21st time McGwire and Sosa had homered on the same day. "It's unexplainable," McGwire said, "so let's leave it unexplainable."

Asked what he would think if they ended in a tie, McGwire said, "Beautiful. If it's a tie or if I'm ahead or if he's ahead, look at what we've done this year. People have been saying for 37 years, 'Can this record be broken?' And two guys have done it. How can you go wrong there?"

The relaxed McGwire capped the historic season with a bang, thrilling the St. Louis fans with two homers on Saturday and two more on the final day to finish with 70. Sosa's total remained at 66.

McGwire's 20-inch biceps and 17-inch forearms had helped him power baseballs over fences. But he also had to be strong mentally. His path was filled with the distractions of daily interviews, fans and players watching every batting practice, and lines of autograph seekers. Every time he stepped into the batter's box, the fans expected him to hit a home run. When a pitcher walked him, they booed. He walked a National League record 162 times.

The big redhead with the monstrous arms and Herculean swing had captured a nation's attention with his home run heroics. "I didn't get to see Babe Ruth," Pagnozzi said. "I didn't get to see Mickey Mantle. But I'm playing with this guy now. And I'll be proud to tell my kids and my grandkids, 'I saw Mark McGwire hit.'"

His presence boosted attendance at ballparks everywhere, but especially in St. Louis. The Cardinals may have wound up 19 games behind Houston in the National League Central at 83–79, but they drew 3,195,021 and sold out all 14 games in September.

Asked about the chances of his ever topping 70, McGwire said, "I don't know if I want to break my own record. I think I would rather leave it as is."

After the final game and the last question, the mentally and physically exhausted McGwire ducked into a limousine and was whisked to the airport where a police escort guided him onto a jet. He flew home to Long Beach, California, to "go back to living a normal life. I'm just going to sit back and collect my thoughts.

CHRONOLOGY

1963   Born in Pomona, California, October 1.

1984   Drafted by Oakland A's.
        Marries Kathy Williams.

1986   Makes major league debut August 22.
        Hits first major league home run August 25.

1987   Hits 49 home runs to set major league rookie record.
        Son Matthew is born.

1990   Wins first Gold Glove.

1996   Hits 300th career home run June 25.
        Hits 50 or more home runs for first of three consecutive years.

1997   Traded to St. Louis Cardinals July 31.
        Ties record for right-handed batters by hitting 58 home runs.

1998   Hits 400th career home run May 8.
        Hits 62nd home run to break single season record September 8.
        Hits 70th home run September 27.

STATISTICS

OAKLAND A'S, ST. LOUIS CARDINALS

Year	Team	G	AB	R	H	2B	3B	HR	RBI	BB	AVG.
1986	Oak A	18	53	10	10	1	0	3	9	4	.189
1987		151	557	97	161	28	4	49	118	71	.289
1988		155	550	87	143	22	1	32	99	76	.260
1989		143	490	74	113	17	0	33	95	83	.231
1990		156	523	87	123	16	0	39	108	110	.235
1991		154	483	62	97	22	0	22	75	93	.201
1992		139	467	87	125	22	0	42	104	90	.268
1993		27	84	16	28	6	0	9	24	21	.333
1994		47	135	26	34	3	0	9	25	37	.252
1995		104	317	75	87	13	0	39	90	88	.274
1996		130	423	104	132	21	0	52	113	116	.312
1997	Oak A	105	366	48	104	24	0	34	81	58	.284
	StL N	51	174	38	44	3	0	24	42	43	.253
	Total	156	540	86	148	27	0	58	123	101	.274
1998	StL N	155	509	130	152	21	0	70	147	162	.299
Totals		**1535**	**5131**	**941**	**1353**	**219**	**5**	**457**	**1130**	**1052**	**.264**

World Series		G	AB	R	H	2B	3B	HR	RBI	BB	AVG.
1988		5	17	1	1	0	0	1	1	3	.059
1989		4	17	0	5	1	0	0	1	1	.294
1990		4	14	1	3	0	0	0	0	2	.214
Totals		**13**	**48**	**2**	**9**	**1**	**0**	**1**	**2**	**6**	**.188**

60

FURTHER READING

Joseph, Paul. *Oakland Athletics*. Minneapolis, MN: Abdo & Daughters, 1997.

Rains, Rob. *Mark McGwire "Mac Attack."* Champaign, IL: Sports Publishing, 1998.

Rains, Rob. *Mark McGwire "Slugger."* Champaign, IL: Sports Publishing, 1998.

Rambeck, Richard. *Oakland A's*. Mankato, MN: Creative Education. 1998.

Mark McGwire – 1998 Home Runs

Number	Date	Opponent	Pitcher	Number	Date	Opponent	Pitcher
1	3/31	vs. LA	Ramon Martinez	36	6/27	at Min	Mike Trombley
2	4/2	vs. LA	Frank Lankford	37	6/30	vs. KC	Glendon Rusch
3	4/3	vs. SD	Mark Langston	38	7/11	vs. Hou	Billy Wagner
4	4/4	vs. SD	Don Wengert	39	7/12	vs. Hou	Sean Bergman
5	4/14	vs. Ariz	Jeff Suppan	40	7/12	vs. Hou	Scott Elarton
6	4/14	vs. Ariz	Jeff Suppan	41	7/17	vs. LA	Brian Bohanon
7	4/14	vs. Ariz	Barry Manuel	42	7/17	vs. LA	Antonio Osuna
8	4/17	vs. Phil	Matt Whiteside	43	7/20	at SD	Brian Boehringer
9	4/21	at Mont	Trey Moore	44	7/26	at Col	John Thomson
10	4/25	at Phil	Jerry Spradlin	45	7/28	vs. Milw	Mike Myers
11	4/30	at ChiCubs	Marc Pisciotta	46	8/8	vs. ChiCubs	Mark Clark
12	5/1	at ChiCubs	Rod Beck	47	8/11	vs. NYMets	Bobby Jones
13	5/8	at NYMets	Rick Reed	48	8/19	at ChiCubs	Matt Karchner
14	5/12	vs. Milw	Paul Wagner	49	8/19	at ChiCubs	Terry Mulholland
15	5/14	vs. Atl	Kevin Millwood	50	8/20	at NYMets	Rick Reed
16	5/16	vs. Fla	Livan Hernandez	51	8/20	at NYMets	Willie Blair
17	5/18	vs. Fla	Jesus Sanchez	52	8/22	at Pit	Francisco Cordova
18	5/19	at Phil	Tyler Green	53	8/23	at Pit	Ricardo Rincon
19	5/19	at Phil	Tyler Green	54	8/26	vs. Fla	Justin Speier
20	5/19	at Phil	Wayne Gomes	55	8/30	vs. Atl	Dennis Martinez
21	5/22	vs. SF	Mark Gardner	56	9/1	at Fla	Livan Hernandez
22	5/23	vs. SF	Rich Rodriguez	57	9/1	at Fla	Donn Pall
23	5/23	vs. SF	John Johnstone	58	9/2	at Fla	Brian Edmondson
24	5/24	vs. SF	Robb Nen	59	9/2	at Fla	Robby Stanifer
25	5/25	vs. Col	John Thomson	60	9/5	vs. Cin	Dennis Reyes
26	5/29	at SD	Dan Miceli	61	9/7	vs. ChiCubs	Mike Morgan
27	5/30	at SD	Andy Ashby	62	9/8	vs. ChiCubs	Steve Trachsel
28	6/5	vs. SF	Orel Hershiser	63	9/15	vs. Pit	Jason Christiansen
29	6/8	at ChiSox	Jason Bere	64	9/18	vs. Mil	Rafael Roque
30	6/10	at ChiSox	Jim Parque	65	9/20	vs. Mil	Scott Karl
31	6/12	at Ariz	Andy Benes	66	9/25	vs. Mon	Shayne Bennett
32	6/17	at Hou	Jose Lima	67	9/26	vs. Mon	Dustin Hermanson
33	6/18	at Hou	Shane Reynolds	68	9/26	vs. Mon	Kirk Bullinger
34	6/24	at Cle	Jaret Wright	69	9/27	vs. Mon	Mike Thurman
35	6/25	at Cle	Dave Burba	70	9/27	vs. Mon	Carl Pavano

INDEX

PICTURE CREDITS
Associated Press/Wide World Photos: pp. 2, 8, 13, 24, 26, 30, 33, 36, 40, 45, 48, 55, 56, 58; Babe Ruth Museum: pp. 29, 51; courtesy of Minnesota Twins: p. 20; Transcendental Graphics: p. 10; USC Athletics: pp. 16, 18

CARRIE MUSKAT has covered major league baseball since 1981, beginning with United Press International in Minneapolis. She was UPI's lead writer at the 1991 World Series. A freelance journalist since 1992, she is a regular contributor to *USA Today* and *USA Today Baseball Weekly.* Her work also has appeared in the *Chicago Tribune, Athlon Sports, Inside Sports* and *ESPN Total Sports* magazine. She has written children's books on Frank Thomas, Barry Bonds, Sammy Sosa, and Moises Alou.

JIM MURRAY, who passed away in 1998, was a veteran sports columnist of the *Los Angeles Times,* and one of America's most acclaimed writers. He was named "America's Best Sportswriter" by the National Association of Sportscasters and Sportswriters 14 times, was awarded the Red Smith Award, and was twice winner of the National Headliner Award. In addition, he was awarded the J. G. Taylor Spink Award in 1987 for "meritorious contributions to baseball writing." With this award came his 1988 induction into the National Baseball Hall of Fame in Cooperstown, New York. In 1990, Jim Murray was awarded the Pulitzer Prize for Commentary.

EARL WEAVER is the winningest manager in the Baltimore Orioles' history by a wide margin. He compiled 1,480 victories in his 17 years at the helm. After managing eight different minor league teams, he was given the chance to lead the Orioles in 1968. Under his leadership the Orioles finished lower than second place in the American League East only four times in 17 years. One of only 12 managers in big league history to have managed in four or more World Series, Earl was named Manager of the Year in 1979. The popular Weaver had his number, 5, retired in 1982, joining Brooks Robinson, Frank Robinson, and Jim Palmer, whose numbers were retired previously. Earl Weaver continues his association with the professional baseball scene by writing, broadcasting, and coaching.